MY
MiNDFUL
MiND

BE
PRESENT
IN EVERY
MOMENT

CLEAR OUT YOUR MIND CLUTTER.

Write, paint, scribble, sketch... whatever you like,
until your head feels a little more spacious...

HAPPY THOUGHTS

Things I'm grateful for:

_____

_____

_____

_____

_____

_____

_____

Things to get done:

_____

_____

_____

_____

_____

_____

_____

WHAT'S ON YOUR MIND TODAY?

My hopes :

_____

_____

_____

_____

_____

_____

_____

My fears:

_____

_____

_____

_____

_____

_____

_____

KIND THOUGHTS

POSITIVE THOUGHTS

CALL A CLOSE FRIEND

Dedicate some distraction-free time
to the call and really listen to them:

· How is their tone of voice?

· Are they excited ? Worried?

· Do they have some big dates coming up?

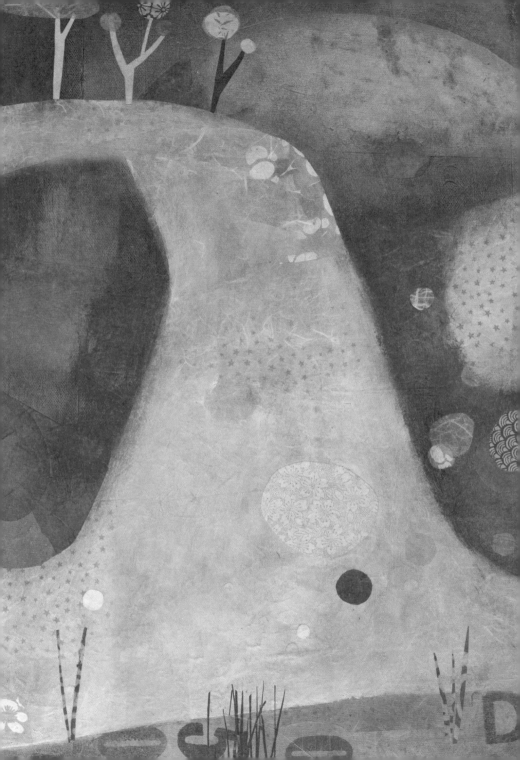

TAKE A DIFFERENT
route TO WORK
TODAY...

Write down all the new things you notice:

_____

_____

_____

_____

_____

_____

_____

_____

_____

_____

_____

_____

The things you LOVE most about YOU...

_____

_____

_____

_____

_____

_____

_____

_____

_____

_____

_____

_____

_____

_____

_____

_____

_____

_____

_____

TAKE A
MOMENT

Lay back, close your eyes
and imagine you're on a deserted beach...

...the sand between your toes...

...the sun on your skin...

...the salty sea air...

Note the sensations and how it made you feel.

TRY MINDFUL EATING...

Turn off all distractions (phone, tv, music)

Sit at a table

Allow enough time (don't rush)

Close your eyes

Chew slowly

Write about it

What I'm eating: _____

The aroma: _____

The taste: _____

The texture: _____

What I'm eating: _____

The aroma: _____

The taste: _____

The texture: _____

What I'm eating: _____

The aroma: _____

The taste: _____

The texture: _____

What I'm eating: _____

The aroma: _____

The taste: _____

The texture: _____

I
CAN'T
CONTROL
WHAT HAPPENS
TO ME, BUT I CAN
CONTROL
HOW I REACT
TO IT.

_____

_____

_____

_____

_____

_____

_____

_____

_____

_____

_____

_____

_____

_____

_____

_____

_____

_____

_____

SuNNY THOUGHTS

HOW ARE YOU FEELING TODAY?

_____

_____

_____

_____

_____

_____

_____

_____

_____

_____

_____

_____

THiS MONTH'S MiNDFULNESS GOALS

POSITIVE THOUGHTS

LET GO OF WHAT YOU CAN'T CHANGE

Draw the view from your window right now...

Write a list of things in the past
that you would like to LET GO of...

_____

_____

_____

_____

_____

_____

_____

_____

_____

_____

_____

_____

_____

_____

_____

LiVE
HeRE...

Write a list of things
you're LOOKING FORWARD to...

→ THE
PRESENT

HAPPY THOUGHTS

SIMPLY BE WHERE YOU ARE.

MINDFULNESS 5-4-3-2-1

Write down...

5 things you can see

_____

_____

4 things you can feel

_____

_____

3 things you can smell

_____

_____

2 things you can hear

_____

_____

1 thing you can taste

_____

_____

TAKE A SOLO WALK...

Note the feelings, smells, sights and sounds you encounter

_____
_____
_____
_____
_____
_____
_____

Instead of taking a photo, describe or draw your favourite view on the walk:

Things I'm grateful for:

_____

_____

_____

_____

_____

_____

_____

Things to get done:

_____

_____

_____

_____

_____

_____

_____

WHAT'S ON YOUR MIND TODAY?

My hopes :

_____

_____

_____

_____

_____

_____

_____

My fears:

_____

_____

_____

_____

_____

_____

_____

KIND THOUGHTS

I WILL LET ANY WORRIES THAT COME AROUND BE ACKNOWLEDGED, THEN DRIFT AWAY LIKE a CLOUD.

WRITE YOUR NEGATIVE THOUGHTS IN THESE BALLOONS...

THEN LET THEM GO!

PUT ON YOUR FAVOURITE FEEL-GOOD SONG, TURN UP THE VOLUME & DANCE LIKE NOBODY'S WATCHING!

POSITIVE THOUGHTS

Things I'm grateful for:

_____

_____

_____

_____

_____

_____

_____

Things to get done:

_____

_____

_____

_____

_____

_____

_____

WHAT'S ON YOUR MIND TODAY?

My hopes :

_____

_____

_____

_____

_____

_____

_____

My fears:

_____

_____

_____

_____

_____

_____

_____

HAPPY THOUGHTS

TODAY iS THE DAY

YOU HAVE five MINUTES TO WORRY TODAY...

Starting now. Write it all down. Then you're done.

_____

_____

_____

_____

_____

_____

_____

_____

_____

_____

_____

_____

_____

_____

_____

_____

STOP FOR A MOMENT

Write down all the things you can hear right now...

_____

_____

_____

_____

_____

_____

_____

_____

_____

_____

_____

_____

_____

_____

TAKE A MOMENT TO THINK...

What are you grateful for today...?

_____
_____
_____
_____
_____
_____
_____
_____
_____
_____
_____
_____
_____
_____
_____
_____
_____
_____

CHOOSE A SONG

CLOSE your eyes. LISTEN to every word.

THE THINGS THAT MAKE MY LIFE GOOD...

WHAT HAVE YOU GOT PLANNED TODAY?
Mark down times and plans.

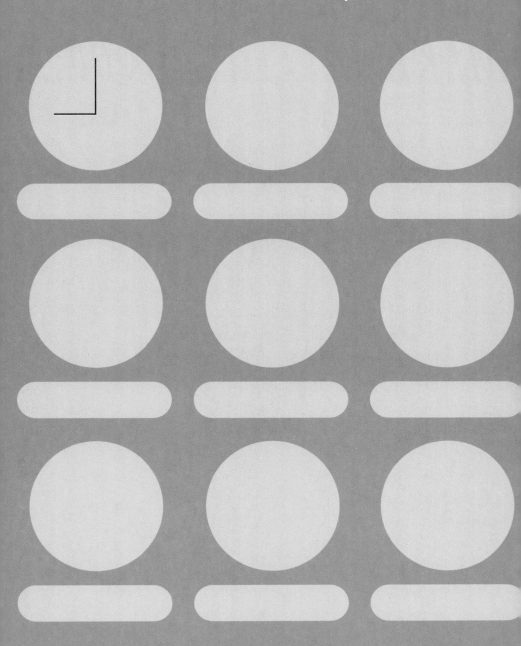

Then get rid of something. Make some time for yourself!

A LiTTLE
PROGRESS
EACH DAY
CREATES BiG
RESULTS

Things I'm grateful for:

_____

_____

_____

_____

_____

_____

_____

Things to get done:

_____

_____

_____

_____

_____

_____

_____

WHAT'S ON YOUR MIND TODAY?

My hopes :

_____

_____

_____

_____

_____

_____

My fears:

_____

_____

_____

_____

_____

_____

KIND THOUGHTS

WHAT HAPPENED TODAY?

SUNNY THOUGHTS

WHEN YOU'RE
TIRED,
DON'T QUIT,
JUST REST.

minDFuL THOUGHTS

STOP FOR A MOMENT.

Write down all the things you can smell right now...

_____

_____

_____

_____

_____

_____

_____

_____

_____

_____

_____

_____

_____

_____

_____

_____

_____

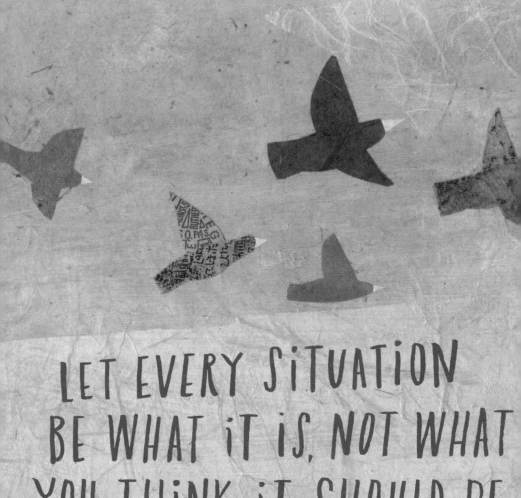

LET EVERY SITUATION
BE WHAT IT IS, NOT WHAT
YOU THINK IT SHOULD BE.

WHAT ARE YOU THINKING RIGHT NOW?

_____

_____

_____

_____

_____

_____

_____

_____

_____

_____

_____

_____

_____

_____

LIST THE THINGS YOU LOVE TO DO...

_____

_____

_____

_____

_____

_____

_____

_____

_____

_____

_____

_____

_____

...can you make time for one of them today?

APPRECIATE EVERY LITTLE THING.

Things I'm grateful for:

_____

_____

_____

_____

_____

_____

_____

Things to get done:

_____

_____

_____

_____

_____

_____

_____

WHAT'S ON YOUR MIND TODAY?

My hopes :

_____

_____

_____

_____

_____

_____

My fears:

_____

_____

_____

_____

_____

_____

POSITIVE THOUGHTS

GOOD THOUGHTS

WHAT I KNOW ABOUT MYSELF...

When I'm HAPPY I...

_____

_____

_____

_____

_____

_____

_____

When I'm SAD I...

_____

_____

_____

_____

_____

_____

_____

SUNNY THOUGHTS

DO LESS, FOCUS MORE.

mindful THOUGHTS

KIND THOUGHTS

WHAT CONTROLS YOUR MIND CONTROLS YOUR Life. LET it GO.

Things I'm grateful for:

_____

_____

_____

_____

_____

_____

_____

Things to get done:

_____

_____

_____

_____

_____

_____

_____

WHAT'S ON YOUR MIND TODAY?

My hopes :

_____

_____

_____

_____

_____

_____

My fears:

_____

_____

_____

_____

_____

_____

HAPPY THOUGHTS

WRITE 10 POSITIVE THINGS ABOUT YOURSELF HERE...

1. _____

2. _____

3. _____

4. _____

5. _____

6. _____

7. _____

8. _____

9. _____

10. _____

TAKE THE
TIME TO DO
WHAT MAKES
YOUR SOUL
HAPPY

SUNNY THOUGHTS

MINDFUL THOUGHTS